SUSAN SAYERS
NOT ANOTHER CAROL SERVICE

Alternative Christmas Workshops
for All-Age Outreach

Kevin Mayhew

First published in 1996 by
KEVIN MAYHEW LTD
Rattlesden
Bury St Edmunds
Suffolk IP30 0SZ

0 1 2 3 4 5 6 7 8 9

ISBN 0 86209 869 6
Catalogue No 1500061

Cover illustration by Claire Boyce
Inside illustrations by Jennifer Carter
Typesetting by Louise Hill
Printed in Great Britain by
Caligraving Limited Thetford Norfolk

Contents

Foreword

Christmas offers the Church a phenomenal opportunity for outreach. However we may feel about the scale and materialism of the traditional festivities, the fact remains that many people are willing to walk into church buildings at this time of year, drawn by nostalgia, perhaps, or a Christmas card sense that these places are part of the seasonal magic. It is one of those times when it is seen as acceptable for your children to be 'doing something at the church'; and at a deeper level, it is full of possibility for jaded and cluttered lives to be sensitised once again.

The ideas for these workshops and Christmas services grew out of a longing to use the opportunity we have been given. Whatever people thought they were coming to see, I wanted them to be awakened to the possibility of the real God, fully alive, rather than a traditionally sentimental presentation of a story from their childhood. I felt that what we did had to be just as important for the adults as the children, and I wanted us all to explore the extraordinary nature of the Incarnation – 'God with us' – rather than dwelling entirely on the nativity.

On the practical side, the rehearsing of any presentation can turn out to be a big headache in the weeks leading up to Christmas, when you are competing with colds and flu, carol services, end of term concerts and so on. Rarely is your entire cast present at any one rehearsal, and you may well find that the cast available on the night is lacking its star roles through illness or unexpected family commitments.

One year I decided to try things differently.

Forget all those rehearsals. Why not have a workshop on Christmas Eve itself for the afternoon, offering parents the chance to get on with all their pre-Christmas secrets, and the children something positive to do to use up some of their energy and excitement? Parents and friends could then be invited to the resulting presentation and service, lasting no more than half an hour and suitable for all ages.

Provided a small core team of leaders is fully prepared, the entire presentation, complete with music, costumes and props, can be completed in the afternoon, and the children enjoy the challenge of starting from scratch like this. There is a freshness about the performance which gets lost in frequently rehearsed plays, and the expectations are different, so that the whole thing becomes lighter and more fun to do.

Obviously this format does not allow for a traditional script with lines to be learnt. Instead there are various techniques used, including tapes, narrators and even voice-overs. All the presentations involve the congregation and are in the context of worship. They would work with any sized group from fifteen upwards, as they have been planned without prior knowledge of numbers, and are necessarily flexible.

I have included a section on the practicalities of planning and running the workshop, and all the ingredients to help you put together the presentation in the context of a crib service. There is of course no need to stick rigidly to these suggestions; for some they will simply provide the ideas to start you off on something completely different.

SUSAN SAYERS

Running a Christmas Workshop

STAGE 1 Pray

Invite everyone in the church to pray, either through the weekly handout or through prayer and Bible study groups. It is important that the whole community is involved.

Get in touch with God's agenda and concerns before you start organising anything, as he is in a far better position to know the needs of those who will eventually be coming.

Invite some people (the elderly and housebound, perhaps) to volunteer prayer support for the entire time the workshop and service will be running.

STAGE 2 Browse

Read through the scripts in God's company, bearing in mind the families in your area, before deciding on which one to use this year. Make a note of any adaptations that may spring to mind.

STAGE 3 Leaders' planning

Make copies of the script for everyone and read through them together.

Decide who is going to take responsibility for what.

Checklist
- Teaching the acting
- Teaching the music
- Special effects
- Advertising and registration
- Copying and OHP
- Budget
- Costumes
- Art and craft
- Refreshments
- Furniture arranging
- First Aid
- Young leaders

It's quite a long list, but the key to running a workshop and staying sane is making sure you delegate, so that no one person has too much to do.

STAGE 4 Advertising

Either design your own posters or use the suggestions at the beginning of each workshop, filling in details as appropriate.

If your church sends a Christmas card, have the workshop included on that.

Ask if you can display details of the event at the local school, or mention it at an assembly.

Contact any clubs which use the church hall and ask if you could come and tell the children about the workshop. Give out leaflets so the messages reach home.

The posters provided on pages 8, 28, 40 and 50 could be reduced for this purpose.

STAGE 5 Timetable

Plan a detailed timetable which is realistic, allowing time for the hidden extras, such as visits to the toilet, moving from one area to another, and putting on outdoor clothes. Here is a possible timetable, to be adapted to your own needs.

1.00pm	Registration
1.15pm	Introduction and singing
1.30pm	First run through
2.15pm	Refreshments
2.25pm	Costumes and props making
2.45pm	Practice of particular sections/ art and craft
3.00pm	Second run through
3.30pm	Refreshments, toilets and quiet game
3.45pm	Dressing up and action stations
4.00pm	Service and presentation begin

THE BETHLEHEM HERALD

–A Christmas Play

To be performed at

on

All Welcome!

Script One

The Bethlehem Herald

As people approach the church they find they are being taken back through the centuries, until by the time they reach the church door they are in Roman-occupied Bethlehem nearly 2000 years ago. Roman soldiers patrol the crowds, and everyone is given official papers for some kind of register. No one is more surprised than Ted Watkinson, a newspaper reporter, who had come to the local church expecting to report on a crib service, and now snatches the opportunity for a scoop story of this time blip. He starts interviewing the soldiers and the Bethlehem crowds, and it is through these interviews that the extraordinary events of Christmas are unfolded.

A group of hidden adults with a microphone provide voice-overs for those being interviewed, and Ted Watkinson will also benefit from using a microphone, preferably a radio mike. He has his script on his clipboard, so no one has words to learn. His camera person can go round with him taking real photographs or video, so that there is a record of the event. Alternatively a junk video camera can be made in advance.

SETTING

Roman-occupied Bethlehem BC. There are crowds of visitors in the city. Roman soldiers are keeping the peace.

Ted Watkinson, reporter for the *Herald* newspaper, has come to (St. Margaret's) crib service, (1996), only to find that an astonishing phenomenon has occurred.

There seems to be a time blip, which has brought everyone at (St. Margaret's) into occupied Bethlehem instead of the crib service they were expecting. Ted Watkinson seizes the opportunity to report on this scoop story.

CAST LIST

- Ted Watkinson, reporter (male or female)
- Residents and visitors in Bethlehem
- Group of soldiers
- Date trader
- Joseph
- Mary
- Inn keeper
- Inn guests
- Servant girl
- Shepherds
- Gabriel
- Angels
- Wise men

PRODUCTION GUIDELINES

1 The voice overs

There are 13 interviews altogether, involving 12 different voices. You will need four or five people to provide these. It works well if you have an older man and woman, and a young man and woman to provide the contrasts. I have given a brief description of each character to get the imagination going. Choose readers who don't mind varying their accent to suit the occasion.

Interview 1
Character — Soldier (male) rough, but proud of his job and aware of his authority.

Interview 2
Character — Date trader (male/female) delighted at the rush of trade.

Interview 3
Character — Old resident (female) slow, warm, comforting, matriarchal.

Interview 4
Character — Traveller (male) young businessman, well-educated.

Interview 5
Character — Joseph and Mary (male and female) Joseph aware of his responsibilities and conscientious. Mary cheerful and practical, but tired.

Interview 6
Character — Inn guest (female) speaks with

distinct dialect (Cockney, or Scottish, perhaps), very appreciative.

Interview 7
Character   Inn keeper (male) traditional family man, efficient and keen to run a good business.

Interview 8 and 10
Character   Servant girl (female) bubbly and chatty. Flustered and excited.

Interview 9
Character   Inn guest (male) tough and outspoken.

Interview 11
Character   Shepherd (male) elderly and with a country dialect of some kind. Bowled over by what he's seen and tickled pink by it all.

Interview 12
Character   Gabriel (male/female) sensible, friendly and patient, with great love and affection for God.

Interview 13
Character   Wise man (male) very intelligent, learned, and a little irritated by woolly thinkers. Speaks in a thoughtful, measured way.

Give the voice-overs their scripts in good time before the performance and have one session together before the actual day to check volume, pace and expression. Make sure they don't speak too fast. They will not necessarily have to be at the whole workshop.

2 Costumes

If you already have a set of traditional costumes you can use these for the characters concerned. It is a very good resource to have, and worth investing some time to produce. If you gather together a group of dressmakers, beg for old curtains and sheets, and frequent a few charity shops and jumble sales, you can create a set of traditional nativity costumes without too much hard work for any one person. Make simple, loose fitting tunics, wraps and cloaks, with belts and girdles.

If you are working only with the workshop in mind, cut long tabards from different materials which can be worn over the children's clothes and tied around the waist. There is no need to stitch these for a single wearing. Ask each child to bring with them a teatowel or cloth head-covering, and a small blanket or cloak.

Have some small baskets and cloth bundles ready to give out to travellers, sticks for the shepherds and spray-painted boxes for the wise men's gifts. Thick curtains can be used to make simple cloaks for the wise men.

For the soldiers, buy, beg or borrow some XL white teeshirts for the tunics. Cut the basic shape of the armour from old sheets, using the pattern on page 12. These can be spray-painted with metalic paint and worn over the tunics. The helmets are made by cutting out the pattern in thick brown wrapping paper, stapling together the flaps at the top centre, and spray-painting. Lengths of brown or black wool are then criss-crossed round the lower leg. The Centurion can wear a short red cape as well.

Angels will have tabards made from sheeting, with tinsel round the head. Suggestions for the manufacture of costumes will be found on page 12.

3 Props and lighting

The action can take place wherever is most convenient in the type of building you are using. One possibility, if you have moveable seating, is to turn the seats round to face in towards the central aisle. This creates a central 'street', so that the crowd can bustle up and down it, and move to one end for the inn, leaving the other end free for the shepherds, wise men and angels. Whatever you decide, ensure that people can see as much as possible.

In some churches there is a possibility of spotlighting certain areas. If this is feasible, light the section of the church where the action takes place, and have full lighting on for the carols in between the interviews.

A manger can be a wooden vegetable box with straw inside. The star can be made of card, covered in foil and fixed on to a beanstick. It can then be carried along in front of the wise men and Ted Watkinson on their way to the inn.

Paint the words of 'The sky is filled with the glory of God' on a cloud-shaped piece of white sheeting, so that it can be draped over a balcony as the angels appear behind it. Alternately, draw a cloud shape behind the words on an OHP acetate and display either on the screen or on an area of wall or ceiling. (Please see section on page 60 regarding copyright.)

It is effective to have this track played on tape to accompany everyone's singing.

4 Crowd control

Since there is a lot to fit in during the available time, you need to avoid disruptions and upsets by good organisation. It is far simpler to label the children with their parts as they arrive, rather than spending time selecting and auditioning once they are there. Freezer labels are wonderfully useful here.

Beforehand number your freezer labels 1, 2 and 3 in equal amounts. Other labels have initials on them to denote particular characters. As the children register, tick them off and give them a number. Also give out the character labels, writing these beside the names on the register in case of lost labels or memory loss.

Ask the 1s to find a space in the central 'street' and sit down in twos and threes.

Ask the 2s to find some spaces and stand in groups of two or three. Ask the 3s to walk up and down and round about between the others. The effect is of a busy street.

Similarly in the inn, the 1s can be eating and drinking, the 2s lying asleep, and the 3s sitting in groups chatting or playing with dice.

The soldiers are shown their patrol route around the church, and keep walking round it, stopping to check people now and again.

5 The interviews

Explain to the children that when Ted Watkinson interviews them, they need to look as if they are answering him, but they will hear the words coming from somewhere else.

It is important that Ted Watkinson is a colourful, friendly and encouraging person, able to ad lib where necessary if any of the children forget where they are supposed to be.

6 Music

(For a complete list of sources please see page 60)

O little town of Bethlehem
Little donkey
In the bleak mid-winter
Silent night, holy night
The sky is filled
See him lying on a bed of straw
Our God is so big
We three kings

7 Artwork

To give the congregation the sense of travelling back in time, have a series of pictures forming a time-line, either outside the church or, in wet weather, just inside. These can be either on lengths of wallpaper, or strips of cloth. Have the pictures outlined beforehand, and the children can work on the painting, several to a picture. Some ideas for pictures are given on pages 13 to 18, but of course you may have much better ideas of your own.

Soldiers will be making their helmets. Other children will be making money, from thin card and foil. Others will make lanterns.

The BEATLES 1966

FIRE OF LONDON
— 1666 —

HAROLD REX

BATTLE of HASTINGS 1066

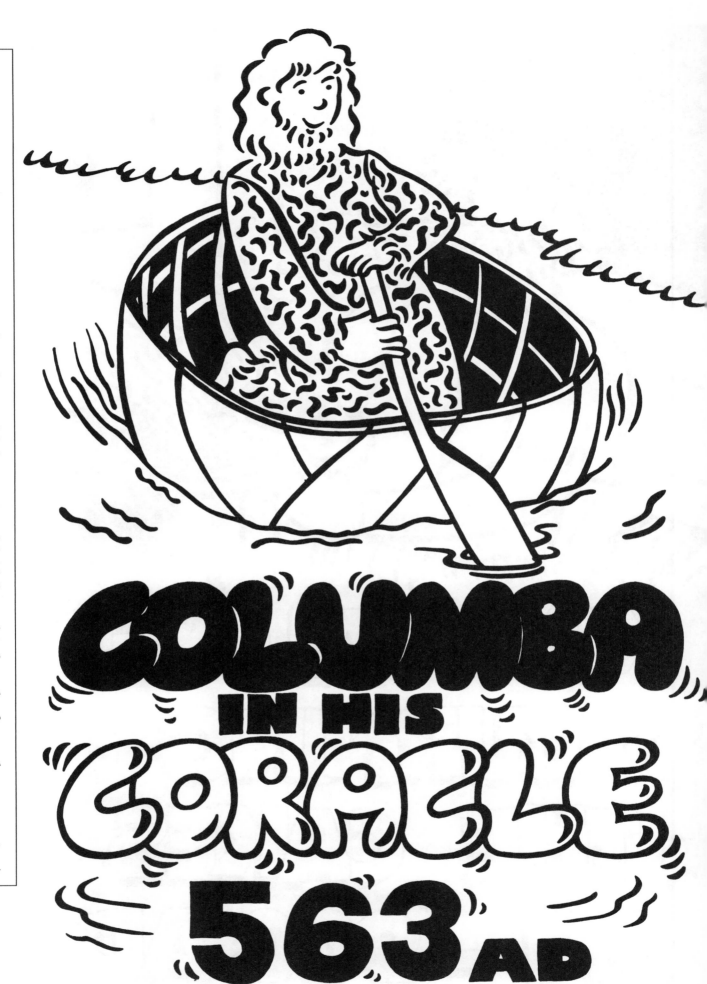

Script

The Interviews

1. A Roman soldier

TW	Bethlehem seems to be packed full of people tonight. Why are there so many people here?
Soldier	Well, if their family roots are in Bethlehem, that's where they have to come for the register.
TW	What register is this?
Soldier	What register? Where have you been, sunshine? THE register, I'm talking about, ordered by Caesar Augustus, so he can find out exactly how many people there are in this part of the Roman Empire. Where were you born, yourself?
TW	(South Benfleet in Essex)
Soldier	Never heard of it. It must be in another province.
TW	Yes, you could say that.
Soldier	Well, if I were you I'd get yourself over there sharpish if you don't want to end up on the wrong side of the law.
TW	Have there been many people breaking the law with these crowds?
Soldier	A few fights and some pickpockets of course. Nothing too serious. Nothing the Roman army can't cope with. *(To a traveller)* Get a move on there!
TW	Well, the Roman army appears to have full control over the city of Bethlehem tonight.

Carol: *O little town of Bethlehem* Verse 1

2. A date trader

TW	You sell dates, I see. Tell me, how do you feel about all these strangers coming to your city for the register?
Trader	Suits me very well. Caesar can have another register next year if he wants to. I haven't sold so many dates in years!

19

3. An old resident

TW	What about you, madam; how do you feel about all these strangers?
Resident	Oh, there aren't many strangers, you know. Most of them are cousins and grandchildren we haven't seen since they moved away. It's so exciting to meet up again.
TW	Where are they all staying?
Resident	Well, our house is so full it's nearly splitting at the seams. And there's three new grandchildren I've never met before, as they were born after my son moved from here. I've just had to come out to buy some extra bread.

4. A traveller

TW	Good evening, sir. You seem to have a fair bit of luggage with you. Where have you come from?
Traveller	I've travelled from Jericho – that's getting on for 25 miles.
TW	How long has it taken you to get here?
Traveller	Two days. I'll be glad of some shelter and a hot meal tonight.
TW	Where will you be staying while you're in Bethlehem?
Traveller	There's a good inn in Fish Street I used to drink at when I lived here; I shall be meeting up with my old school friends and catching up on the news.
TW	Sounds like a pleasant evening, sir.

5. Joseph and Mary

TW	Here's someone else who's travelled some distance, by the look of it. Good evening, sir; where have you come from?
Joseph	Good evening. My wife and I have come from the city of Nazareth.

TW	How many miles is that?
Joseph	It's about 75 miles away from here. It took us nearly a week to get here as my wife is not up to walking at her usual speed at the moment. The baby is due to be born soon, you see.
TW	Have you got relatives here to stay with?
Joseph	There's plenty of relatives, but they all have lots of visitors already staying with them. We're hoping the inn will be able to put us up. The inn keeper is a distant cousin of mine.
TW	How did you find the journey, madam, in your condition?
Mary	Well, we made it, and God has looked after us and kept us safe, I'm happy to say. But I'm glad we can rest now.
TW	I hope all goes well for you both – and the baby when it arrives.
Mary	Thank you.

Carol: *Little donkey*

(The crowds move to the front of the church (the inn) where some are sleeping, some sit chatting, and some are eating and drinking. Servants and the inn keeper move among them, with jugs and bowls.)

6. An inn guest (female)

TW	I'm standing in one of the inns in the city of Bethlehem, and it looks to me to be a bit overcrowded, to say the least. There are people sleeping, eating, drinking, and just passing the time. I wonder what they think of the service they are getting at this place. *(Goes to a woman)* Excuse me, madam, is this inn cheap to stay in?
Woman	Not a bad price, really. I'm just thankful I've got a roof over my head tonight.
TW	Have you had some food here?
Woman	Yes, I have. They have a pot of soup on all the time, and I

tell you I was ready for it. It was piping hot, and very tasty.

TW So you're satisfied with the service you are getting here?

Woman I certainly am, bless them. They're working flat out and doing a grand job.

7. The inn keeper

TW Good evening, sir. Do you run this inn?

Inn keeper Yes, that's right, I do. And my father ran it before me, God rest his soul. It's a family business, you see.

TW How are you managing with all these extra crowds who have come to be registered?

Inn keeper Well, it's a bit of a headache, but we're doing our best! It's quite a party spirit, really. Lots of them know one another, and haven't seen each other for ages. Augustus Caesar has done us quite a good turn, for once. But don't quote me on that – I'd be in trouble with the Roman authorities.

TW I've just been talking to one couple from Nazareth who are hoping to get a place here. The man said you were a cousin of his.

Inn keeper Ah, that will be Joseph and his wife, Mary. Yes, we're expecting them, though I haven't a clue where they'll fit. But we'll manage, somehow, even if they have to use the annex.

TW What's the annex like?

Inn keeper Oh, it's where we stable the animals and keep the hay. It's quite warm, and it would give them a bit more privacy than in here.

TW That's good – they'll appreciate a bit of privacy if the baby decides to come into the world tonight.

(Mary and Joseph walk up to the inn, greet the inn keeper, and he shows them to the stable. The crowds cover up the entrance to it so they can't be seen.)

Carol: *In the bleak mid-winter*

(A servant girl runs across with a towel and a jug, shouting 'excuse me' to everyone as she pushes past.)

8. Servant girl

TW   Hold on a minute – what's happening? What's all the rush and excitement? What am I missing?

Servant girl   You'll never guess – one of the guests is having a baby. They only arrived this evening – now if you don't mind, I need to get through to her.

TW   Is that the couple who are staying in the stable annex?

Servant girl   Yes, that's right. Now get out of the way. You reporters are all the same!

9. An inn guest (male)

TW   Well, this is most extraordinary. Not only do we find ourselves in occupied Bethlehem, nearly 2000 years ago, but we're actually here when a baby is being born. I must get through and interview Joseph and Mary again.

Man   Oh no you don't. You let them have the baby in peace, for heaven's sake. They don't want the whole world knowing the baby is being born in a stable in Bethlehem.

TW   All right, all right, I suppose you have a point. Do you know Joseph and Mary?

Man   Yes, I know Joseph. He and I lived in the same street when we were children. He was really clever at making things. He became a carpenter when he grew up, you know.

TW   What about Mary – do you know her?

Man   No, she didn't live in Bethlehem – she lived in Nazareth. Fancy them having to make a journey like this with a baby on the way. It's a disgrace.

(The servant girl runs out shouting 'It's a boy, it's a boy!')

10. Servant girl

TW	How is the baby doing?
Servant girl	Oh, he's a beautiful baby boy, he really is!
TW	And what about Mary?
Servant girl	She's pretty tired, of course, but I've made her comfortable and Joseph is looking after her. They're both very happy.
TW	What are they using for a cot for the baby?
Servant girl	Joseph had a really good idea – we've laid the baby in the animals' eating trough.
TW	In an eating trough?
Servant girl	Well, I know it sounds disgusting, but the manger is full of clean hay, so the baby is nice and cosy.
TW	Well, I've never heard of a baby being put in a manger before. Although, wait a minute . . . I think perhaps I have. Surely not!

Carol: *Silent night, holy night*

(At the other end of the church, a group of shepherds are standing. A group of angels stand ready, either up in the balcony, or on a table nearby. Suddenly the clouds above them are lit up and everyone sings: 'The sky is filled with the glory of God'. TW walks briskly down to the shepherds as the angels disappear and walk up the side of the church to be ready at the inn after the next carol.)

11. The shepherd

TW	This is incredible – first Bethlehem instead of (St. Margaret's) crib service, then a baby being born and put in a manger, and now these extraordinary lights in the sky. It looked as if people of some kind were talking to these shepherds and telling them something. I now bring you live to a hillside just outside Bethlehem. Excuse me, sir, I noticed a lot of lights in the sky just now. Do you know anything about them?

Shepherd	Angels, that's what they were, angels! And talking to me, Ben Barjonah! Whatever will my wife say when I tell her.
TW	Did you say they were talking to you? What about?
Shepherd	They said that God was come among us as a baby. Come to sort us out, he said. It must be the Messiah we've been waiting for all these years. And in my lifetime, too. Would you believe it!
TW	That's interesting. I've just been reporting on a newborn baby.
Shepherd	Not this one, I don't reckon. You see the angel said we'd know which baby it was because he'd be lying in a manger. There can't be many of those around, now can there!
TW	But that's it – the baby I'm talking about *is* in a manger – some travellers came for the register and the inn was so crowded that the stable annex was the only space they could find for this woman to have the baby. Follow me – I can take you straight to it!
Shepherd	Well, bless my beard, there's some strange and wonderful things going on tonight. God, born as a baby! Laid in a manger! Whatever next!

Carol: *See him lying on a bed of straw*

(*The shepherds and TW walk up to the inn. The crowds part and form a group around the family. The shepherds kneel by the manger. Gabriel is there as well, and the angels.*)

12. Gabriel

TW	Here we are, back at the inn in the stable annex, and yes, Mary and Joseph and their baby are settled in quite well. Excuse me, sir, didn't I see you in the sky earlier on, talking to the shepherds?
Gabriel	Yes, that's right. Angels aren't stuck in one place like humans. God sends us wherever we're needed. We're messengers.

TW	Who exactly is this baby?
Gabriel	*(kneels)* This baby is God himself, born to live on earth so he can save the humans he made and loves so much.
TW	But how can God be God, and this baby as well?
Gabriel	YOU couldn't be, of course, but that's only because you're human. Don't make the mistake of thinking God is only a human. He isn't. He's a different being altogether.
TW	What is he like, then?
Gabriel	He's powerful enough to create the universe, *(raises arms)* and humble enough *(extends arms to the baby)* to put all his glory aside so as to live here with us. He's completely full of love, and there is nothing and no one he doesn't notice or care about.
TW	That's amazing. It's all much . . . much bigger than I realised.
Gabriel	Yes. With God, nothing is impossible.

Song: *Our God is so big*

(At the back of the church the wise men arrive. A star shines above them in the sky. TW sees them and walks down to them.)

13. The wise man

TW	I've just noticed some very important-looking visitors to Bethlehem. Let's find out who they are and what they're doing here. Excuse me, sir, may I ask what you are doing in a place like Bethlehem? If you'll forgive me, you seem a bit grand for these parts.
Wise man	Greatness is in a person's character, young man, not his money or his clothes. We have come to find a king who we believe has recently been born.
TW	A king! *(Aside)* Can they mean the God child in the manger? *(To the wise man)* A king, you say. There aren't many palaces here though.

Wise man	Foolish, young man, the king we seek would need no palace. Even the stars proclaim his coming. Has there been an unusual birth near here?
TW	Well, now you come to mention it, yes there certainly has. God even got angel messengers to tell some shepherds about it. And this lot were all brought nearly 2000 years to see him.
Wise man	Now you are talking like a wiser man. Always keep your mind open and the truth will often surprise you.
TW	Yes . . . thanks for the advice. Shall we go to this child, then?
Wise man	Indeed we shall. I want to seek him all my life. Come.

Carol: *We three kings*

(During the carol the wise men and TW are led by the star towards the inn. They wait in the centre aisle until the verses about gold, frankincense and myrrh. In turn they walk slowly up to the manger and present their gifts.)

Now everyone is led in prayer, the Christmas tree lights are switched on and a birthday cake is brought in with a lit candle on it.

Sing 'Happy Birthday to Jesus' and give away slices of cake to everyone before they go home.

Suggestion for prayer

> Living God,
> thank you for coming
> to live among us as a person.
> Thank you for showing us
> so much love.
> Open our eyes
> to notice you this Christmas
> and help us to share your love
> at home and with our friends.
> Amen.

STARBIRTH

–A Christmas Play

To be performed at

on

All Welcome.

Script Two

Starbirth

SETTING

Somewhere out in the universe C.K. is in a spaceship which has just lost contact with ground control. In her panic she asks God to help, and God responds, in the mystery play tradition, talking to her and taking her on a trip round the universe while she waits to have contact re-established.

As she marvels at the wonders of stars, planets and black holes, she also makes friends with their Creator, who helps her understand why there needed to be a rescue plan, and where Jesus being born in Bethlehem fits in with it all.

The children provide all the special effects in this production, changing from swirling galaxies to cosmic winds, solar flares to storms on Jupiter and exploding in light as a new star is born.

The congregation is led to see both the power and majesty of God, and also his affection and love for ordinary people.

CAST LIST

- C.K.
- God
- Ground Control
- Stars
- Mary
- Joseph
- Jesus
- OHP operator
- Spaceship operator team
- Tape recorder operator
- Musician(s)
- Galaxy young leaders

PRODUCTION GUIDELINES

1 Crowd control

The children are divided into small groups of stars to form galaxies. You will need a number of young leaders, in the 12 to 20 age group, one to stick with each small group of children, overseeing their set of props and helping them do the right things at the right times. Each young leader is given a script, a schedule of activities and equipment needed, and a box of equipment. The galaxies establish base camp at different places all around the church, so that whenever the stars are swirling, the members of the congregation feel as if they are in the middle of the universe, surrounded by stars.

Use numbered freezer labels to put the children into groups as they register, and keep a note of these numbers with some spare labels.

2 Props and special effects

Invite a family or a couple of friends to make a spaceship several weeks before the production. Provide them with an empty washing up bottle to give them a starting point and an idea of size, but leave the details to them; children have a remarkable gift for making amazing things out of junk. They may even be able to fit it with lights!

The spaceship will be fixed with tape to strong string, and this is made into a huge loop which can then be moved along so that the spaceship moves as well. Pillars come into their own, here, and if you have a balcony, the loop can go up there. You will need to look at your own building and experiment beforehand.

For the pictures of the planets, the unborn child and the nativity, browse through the library and your Christmas cards to find some clear colour pictures, and take them to an office shop where they can be made into acetates for the OHP. The cost is not high, and you then have an excellent resource for other occasions.

Market shops sell very cheap torches, or you can ask the children to bring their own torches with them.

The bean bags are made in advance from cheap red and orange material (such as old curtains) and either filled with some dried peas, or simply rolled up and knotted. The important thing is that they are reasonably easy to catch, and don't roll too far when dropped.

Bubble mixture can be made from washing-up liquid and water, and kept in a wide-mouthed pot with a lid. Bubble blowers are made in advance by twisting a piece of wire and winding tape round the handle. The young leaders can then hold the bowls as the children gather round and blow their bubbles.

Streamers are made from cutting strips of yellow crêpe paper. They can be kept folded up until they are used.

Animal masks are made from paper plates with the eye holes already cut out. The children design and colour their own masks with crayons or felt pens during the workshop. They simply hold the masks up in front of their faces.

The flowers are small paper plates, cut to shape and coloured by the children. A length of green crêpe paper is stapled on to the back of the flower. To make the flower grow, the children squat down holding their flower and gradually stand up. The green stem will gradually unfold as they do so.

3 Costumes

All the children will be wearing a basic costume made from a black dustbin bag. The heavy duty ones are best. Slits are cut for the head and arms and the edges reinforced with sticky tape to prevent splitting. The back is kept plain, but the children decorate the front of their bags with lengths of tinsel stuck on in swirls with sticky tape.

Mary and Joseph will need cloaks and head-dresses, and their baby can be wrapped in a cloth or small blanket.

4 Music

I have given some suggestions for pieces of music to use, but you may well have different ideas. Decide, in advance, who is going to be responsible for the music so that they have time to get together the recordings that have been chosen.

Instrumental Recordings

2001 Space Odyssey
The Planet Suite – Holst
Carnival of the Animals – Saint-Saëns
Pavanne – Fauré

Songs

(For a complete list of sources, please see page 60)
Father God, you love me
For God so loved the world

You may prefer to have a musician with a keyboard providing some cosmic music throughout the production as and when appropriate, with some of the children accompanying this with percussion instruments and sounds.

5 Actions

The galaxies move slowly round in small circles, holding their torches and their hands joined up.

When the new star is born, they are all facing away from the congregation and swaying and bending, until a given signal, such as a cymbol clashing, when they all jump and twist outwards so that the tinsel on their fronts becomes visible.

The actions to the song *For God so loved the world* are as follows:

For God – point up
so loved the world – trace a circle with open hands, starting with both hands at the top of the circle
he gave his only Son – slowly offer both hands out with palms up
that whoever believes in him – point to yourself and then several other people in turn, then upwards
shall not die – shrink down and put protective hand over head
but have eternal life – stretch both arms upwards and look up
L is for the Love – index finger on opposite palm
that he has for me – hug yourself and swing

30

I am the reason – index finger touches middle finger on opposite hand
he died on the tree – make cross shape with arms
F is for Forgiveness – two fingers crossing two fingers
and now I am free – break the 'F' apart as if breaking out of handcuffs
E is to Enjoy being in his company – dance round on the spot.

The first verse of this song can be sung in harmony with the second, and the children can lead the rest of the congregation.

6 Voices

You will need a good reader to be C.K., either male or female. Decide on this person in advance and let them have the script to practise on.

For God you will need an older, loving and wise voice with a hint of sparkle.

These two will be going through their reading together during the workshop, but may feel they would like to try it before that as well. It is important that they try out the reading with the microphone. This always makes a difference to the speed and pitch, and everyone needs to hear all the words very clearly, as it is the conversation between C.K. and God that gives everyone their cues.

7 Words for 'Who do we believe in?'

Who was there before anything else?
GOD WAS!
Who decided to make our universe?
GOD DID!
Who is in charge of our universe today?
GOD IS!

Who was walking on earth as Jesus?
GOD WAS!
Who loved us so much that he died for us all?
GOD DID!
Who is alive in us now through his Spirit?
GOD IS!
Who do we believe in?
WE BELIEVE IN GOD!

CHECKLIST FOR YOUNG LEADERS

1 Galaxies: swirl, hold hands and circle. (Torches)

2 Birth of star: go to front, seethe, then jump out and turn round.

3 Galaxies: swirl, hold hands and circle. (Torches)

4 Black hole: torches go out. Children freeze. Make wind noise.

5 The sun: go to front, wave yellow streamers. (Streamers)

6 Galaxies: swirl, hold hands and circle. (Torches)

7 Venus: bubble blowing. (Bubble mix and blowers)

8 Jupiter: go to front and throw and catch beanbags. (Beanbags)

9 Galaxies: swirl, hold hands and circle. (Torches)

10 Earth: sing 'Father God, you love me'. (Words displayed on OHP – please see section on page 60 regarding copyright.)

11 Creatures: go to front with masks and parade round church. (Masks)

12 Plants: go to galaxy base and face out to make plants grow. (Plants)

13 People: get into group positions – happy/sad/angry/unkind – and freeze. Then creep slowly to back of church.

14 For God so loved the world: sing at back of church. (Words on OHP – please see section on page 60 regarding copyright.)

15 Baby: walk up to front behind Mary and Joseph and sit for chant. ('Who do we believe in?')

Script
Starbirth

(Music. Darkness. Then lots of small torch lights of stars come on, circling in galaxies all over the church. Spaceship moves to midway of circuit.)

C.K.   Ground control, this is C.K. Are you receiving me? Ground control, where are you? Everything's gone dead. I'm drifting around somewhere in the universe and no hope of getting back home. O God, help me, I'm out of control!

God   Don't worry, I've got you. You're quite safe.

C.K.   How strange – I suddenly feel peaceful inside. Very reassuring . . . That's strange, I think I imagined a voice.

God   Then you imagined right. Want me to show you around while you wait?

C.K.   Show me around? . . . This is crazy, I'm the only one around here. I must be going mad. I thought someone offered to show me around.

God   I did.

C.K.   Who are you? Where are you?

God   Let's just say 'I am.' That answers both questions. But I shouldn't muddle yourself with questions at the moment. You've done enough worrying for one day. Just accept that I'm here and you're safe and I'm offering to show you round the universe.

C.K.   Fair enough, whoever you are. Thanks. Lead on!

God   Hold tight, then. Off we go.

(Music. Spaceship returns to gallery. Children gather in a cluster at front. Spaceship reappears and travels slowly down.)

God   Now watch carefully. You're going to be present at a birth.

C.K.   You mean a baby is being born right out here?

32

God	Not exactly. Certainly not a human baby. But I get excited whenever any of my ideas is born. This birth is a baby star.

(Music. Children seethe together.)

C.K.	Something's happening . . . as if there's loads of energy wanting to explode . . . Good heavens!

(The children turn outwards, jumping up and down and jostling. On their fronts are bright, sparkly swirls.)

C.K.	That's amazing! I can't understand why it doesn't all explode and burst off into space.
God	Good, isn't it? You're quite right, it would explode except for the huge weight of material that it's made of. The laws of physics hold true everywhere in the universe, you see.
C.K.	You seem to know an awful lot about this universe. The way you talk anyone would think you'd made it.
God	Well, I have! I do! And I enjoy every micro-second and light year of it.
C.K.	But if you made it you must be God.
God	That's true. As I said earlier, I am. Come on, let's leave this baby star to shine for a few billion years.

(Music. Spaceship continues down to front and halfway back to gallery. Children go to be galaxies. Music stops. Torches go out. Children make sound of cosmic wind.)

C.K.	It feels weird here – all empty and lost.
God	Yes, it's empty alright. What can you see?
C.K.	Nothing. Nothing at all.
God	That's because we are close to a black hole – all the density

of a huge star that has died, shrunk back into matter which grips light so tightly that nothing can escape from it.

C.K. I'm scared. It's all so huge and powerful.

God Don't be afraid. I am here with you.

C.K. Are you always with us, keeping us company, and leading us safely through the scary times?

God Always. I promise you that. And I always keep my promises.

C.K. I'm going to remember that, when I get back home . . . IF I get back home.

God Come on, we're going to somewhere that should really brighten you up. Hold tight.

(Music. Spaceship goes back to gallery. Children move to front to get yellow streamers. Spaceship approaches front. Sun comes up on OHP. Children shake yellow streamers. Music fades.)

C.K. Oh, it's beautiful – and so brilliant, it's blinding. What a universe!

All WHAT A GOD!

God Lovely, isn't it. It makes me happy to see it working so well.

C.K. People used to worship the sun, didn't they? I can see why. But it seems more logical to worship the one who thought of it in the first place.

God It's always easier to sort out other people's problems, my dear. And I don't stop believing in people just because they don't realise I'm real.

C.K. It's rather hot here. Do you think we could go and see some of the planets in our solar system?

God Why not.

(Music. Children become galaxies. Spaceship goes back to gallery. OHP slide changes to Venus. Children collect bubble mixture and start blowing bubbles and making the wind sounds. Spaceship moves out towards Venus.)

God	Take a guess – where do you think this is?
C.K.	Well, let's see. It's covered with swirling clouds . . . smells of sulphur . . . how about Venus?
God	Well done, very good thinking.

(Music. Spaceship moves back to gallery. OHP slide of Jupiter. Children throw and catch red and orange bean bags. Spaceship moves towards it.)

C.K.	What a universe!
All	WHAT A GOD!
God	This is Jupiter. Another cosmic storm going on by the looks of things.
C.K.	It's amazing that all this is going on while we have tea or do the washing-up.
God	I'm glad you like it. I hoped you would enjoy it. Come on, we're going further away from the sun now.

(Music. OHP slide of Neptune. Children are galaxies. Spaceship continues round to gallery again.)

C.K.	It's Neptune, I think. So cold and blue and alone. What a universe!
All	WHAT A GOD!
C.K.	I'm not sure that I want to go back to earth. It seems rather boring after all this.
God	Not a bit of it. Earth is particularly special and beautiful. It's just that because you're used to it you forget to look at it properly. Come on. I'll show you what I mean. The clouds are lovely at the moment over South America.
C.K.	How do you know? . . . Well, I suppose you know everything, being God. Do you even know what I'm thinking?

God   Oh yes, I've known and loved you since before you were born.

C.K.   I remember singing a song about you when I was at holiday club at (St. Margaret's) once. It seems to make more sense now that I really know you. The words are just coming into my mind . . .

(Song: 'Father God you love me', words on OHP. Music. OHP slide of Earth. Spaceship comes towards it. Children go to front with their creatures at the ready.)

God   Just look at all the different kinds of creatures there are living here.

(Music. Children wear masks and parade around the church.)

C.K.   There may not be any others like that in the rest of the universe. We need to look after all this, don't we?

(Then they take masks off.)

God   And look at the way Earth grows so many different plants and fruit.

(The children make their plants 'grow'.)

And best of all – the people I have made.

(Children freeze in happy/sad/angry positions.)

C.K.   Some of them are unhappy, some are being cruel and unkind.

God Yes, that's true. Sadly, left to themselves, they often get lost.

(Children creep to the back of church.)

C.K. But Father God, that's terrible, when you loved them into life. It's as if they're out of control, like I was when you rescued me.

God There had to be a rescue plan, alright. It meant becoming one of them myself and working from the inside, so to speak.

C.K. But you are Lord of the whole wonderful universe. How could you possibly shrink to human size? And anyway, people can get dangerous. They might kill you, and you are the only One able to give them life!

God That's a risk I had to take. When you love someone you are willing to take risks. And I love the people I have made.

C.K. Listen . . . I can hear singing.

(Children sing 'For God so loved the world'. Words on OHP)

(All dark. Heartbeat, getting louder. OHP slide of unborn child. Nativity OHP slide as baby's cry is heard. Children have been walking slowly up to front behind a Mum, Dad and baby, dressed as Joseph, Mary and Jesus. At the front they turn to face congregation. Children sit. OHP of 'Who do we believe in'.)

Ground control C.K. . . . calling C.K. Are you receiving me? Are you receiving me?

C.K. C.K. to ground control. Receiving you loud and clear. Over!

(Music. Joseph, Mary and Jesus lead all the children round to the crib. Everyone is led in prayer.)

Suggestion for prayer

Father God,
thank you for making our universe.
Help us look after it well.
Thank you for being born as a human baby
and living among us.
Thank you for living with us now.
We welcome you into our homes this Christmas.
Amen.

As the Christmas tree lights are switched on, everyone shouts, 'Jesus is the light of the world!' and claps.

A birthday cake is brought out with a lit candle and everyone sings 'Happy birthday to Jesus'. They receive a slice of cake before they leave.

THE CHRISTMAS PRESENT—

—A Christmas Play

To be performed at

on

All Welcome!

Script Three

The Christmas Present

SETTING

Two children are about to go to bed on Christmas Eve when they notice a huge Christmas present in the corner of the room. When they look into it, they begin to realise it is, quite literally, a Christmas present, as it has Christmas inside it.

No end of characters magically pour out from it, and through each of them the children start to see beyond the materialism and traditions of Christmas to what it is really about.

A narrator and two children read the script, and all the other children mime the different parts. Tapes of music and sounds are used during the production.

CAST LIST

- Narrator
- Andrew (reader)
- Jane (reader)
- Andrew (miming)
- Jane (miming)
- Group of carol singers
- Group of shoppers
- Postman (or several)
- Flock of sheep
- Group of shepherds
- Angels
- Cherub
- Mary
- Joseph
- Jesus

PRODUCTION GUIDELINES

1 Readers

Have an adult voice for the narrator, to contrast with the children's voices. These three readers need to have a script before the workshop, so as to be familiar with it.

Try the reading out with the microphone they will be using, to check for volume and speed, and emphasise the need to speak quite slowly, so that people have time to take in what they are hearing. Since the other children will be taking all their cues from the readers it is essential that they can be heard clearly.

2 Music

Whenever the Christmas present is about to produce something, this is heralded by some music or sound effect. All these can be gathered together in order beforehand, to make things easier for the operator.

You can, of course, vary the sounds to suit your situation, but here are some suggestions:

Introduction
Short piece of 'opening-up music' – perhaps from a musical box.

Track 1 – Carol singers
Record a group of people singing and playing a familiar carol. Or go upmarket and use a track from a cathedral choir.

Track 2 – Shopping
Go to the checkout of a busy local store and ask if you can make a recording. Make sure your tape recorder is close enough to pick up the sound of coins, the till, and the usual checkout conversations.

Track 3 – The postman
Use the Postman Pat theme song.

Track 4 – The sheep
If you live in the country you might want to record some real sheep. Or you may prefer to give people the hint of sheep country with the James Herriot theme music. This track needs to be long enough for the sheep to climb out of the present, and the children to try and catch them, so that it ends with the shepherds climbing out of the box.

Track 5 – The angels
Use a cathedral choir rendering of *Ding dong! merrily on high.*

Track 6 – The cherub
Silent night, holy night. This can either be a recording of your church choir, or you could use a track from a cathedral choir carols

collection. Or you may prefer to have this last track accompanied 'live', using such instruments as keyboard, guitar, xylophone, chime bars or recorders.

3 Other music

(For a complete list of sources, please see page 60)

Clap hands Gloria
God has put his angels
Jesus, Jesus
Shine, Jesus, shine

4 Props and special effects

The Christmas present
For this you will need a very large, firm packing carton, such as a washing machine box, as it has to be big enough for children to climb out of. If you prefer, this could be made from wood.

The back of the box is cut away, a step or stool is placed inside the box, and another step outside, so that the children can creep in from behind when their turn comes, climb on to the step and out into the 'sitting-room'. The children who are acting as Andrew and Jane steady them as they climb out.

If the basic shape is completed beforehand, the children can decorate it with Christmas wrapping paper, ribbon and tinsel during the workshop.

A screen or curtain backdrop is hung, or stands immediately behind the Christmas present, so that all the children can sit behind it until they climb out into the 'sitting-room'. If the design for this is drawn on in advance, one group of children can do the painting during the workshop. Sponge painting covers large areas effectively and quickly.

Thunder
A sheet of card, or a metal tray is shaken and rattled.

5 Costumes

If you have a set of traditional nativity costumes, these can be used for Mary, Joseph

and the baby, the shepherds and the angels. You may be able to use a family with a real baby.

If you are making costumes just for the day, cut out tabards from sheets and curtains and fasten round the waist with cord or string. Have a selection of teacloths and scarves for head coverings. Borrow dressing gowns and lengths of cloth for cloaks.

Andrew and Jane can wear nightclothes over their clothes.

The carol singers wear their outdoor clothes and carry the lanterns made in the workshop using the design on page 12.

The shoppers carry carrier bags from well-known shops, filled out with crumpled newspaper.

Your local sorting office may be willing to lend you a real Royal Mail bag if you ask them nicely and invite them along! Failing that, use a brightly coloured satchel, full of old Christmas cards and used envelopes. Traditional hats are available from toy shops.

For the sheep, ask the children to bring white clothes, and make masks using the design on page 44.

6 Action

There is no need for all the children to be sitting behind the Christmas present all the time. They can sit and watch what is going on, provided they are sitting in the right order, until someone ushers them up just before they are due to emerge from the present.

Andrew and Jane listen to what the readers are saying, and mime what they hear, going over to look inside the Christmas present, and helping out whoever starts to emerge. When the sheep come out they can chase them all over the building. Provide two chairs in the 'sitting-room' so they can sit down when they are not involved in the action.

The carol singers climb out of the box and gather as a group, walking about the church during the singing of *We wish you a merry Christmas*. Then they can sit on the floor to watch the rest until they gather round the family at the end.

The shoppers climb out of the box with

their bags, or pick them up from the box as they come out. The actions and words for their chant are as follows:

Christmas shopping here
(*rush to one side of the aisle*)
Christmas shopping there
(*rush to the other side*)
Only 5 more shopping days to Christmas!
(*hold up 5 fingers*)

Long queues here
(*make a line on one side*)
Long queues there
(*make a line on the other side*)
Only 4 more shopping days to Christmas!
(*hold up 4 fingers*)

Heavy parcels here
(*look weighed down by left side bag*)
Heavy parcels there
(*look weighed down on right side*)
Only 3 more shopping days to Christmas!
(*hold up 3 fingers*)

Grumpy children here
(*stamp feet and look cross*)
Grumpy grown-ups there
(*all shout 'because I say so!'*)
Only 2 more shopping day to Christmas!
(*hold up 2 fingers*)

Sore feet here
(*hobble about on one side of aisle*)
Sore feet there
(*hobble about on other side*)
Only 1 more shopping day to Christmas!
(*hold up 1 finger*)

AND WE'RE EXHAUSTED!
(*Flop in a heap on the floor.*)

The postman/postlady climbs out of the box and walks around the church delivering Christmas cards. Then he/she sits down to watch until it is time to gather round Mary, Joseph and Jesus.

The sheep climb out of the box and run all over the church, bleating. The children try to catch them, but the sheep keep escaping. When the shepherds get out of the box and whistle, all the sheep run to form a flock in front of the shepherds. When the shepherds leave to run down the aisle to the back of the church, the angels take over from the shepherds and lead the sheep to sit down at the side. They can watch the rest of the action until they gather round Mary, Joseph and Jesus at the end.

The angels get out of the box and walk towards the shepherds where they sing the 'Gloria'. Then they go and sit down until it is time to gather round at the end.

The cherub climbs out and runs down to the back, where Mary and Joseph are sitting with Jesus. The cherub leads them up the aisle to the front, and everyone gathers round to make a tableau.

7 Crowd control

Have some freezer labels marked with initials for different parts and, as children arrive to register, work through the labels in rotation, ensuring that all essential parts are allocated, and the group sizes are well-balanced.

Choose someone to demonstrate the magic of the bottomless Christmas present, so they can see how clever it will look to the congregation, but then make this a 'no go' area for everyone, apart from those who will be decorating it. Sit the children in order before the first run through, so the action can flow more easily.

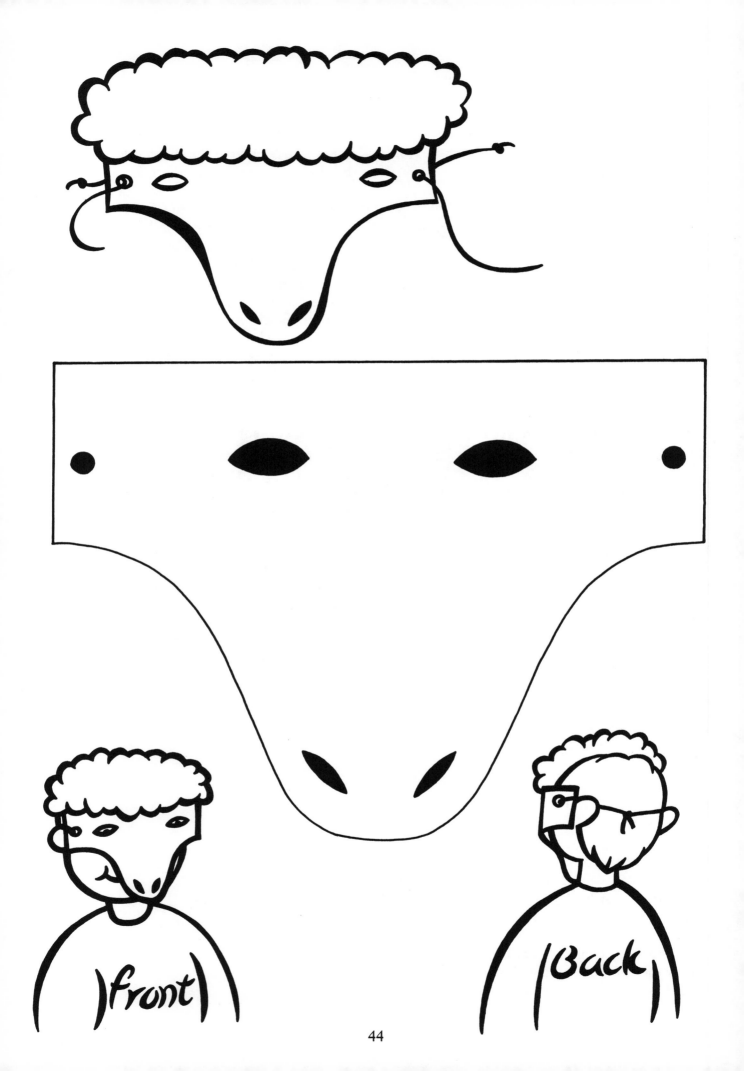

front

Back

Script

The Christmas Present

Narrator	It was the night before Christmas. Christmas Eve. Andrew and Jane were drinking their hot chocolate before going to bed. The room was full of presents ready to open on Christmas day. Suddenly they noticed a huge present they hadn't seen before.
Andrew	What on earth can this be?
Jane	Perhaps it's an elephant in a cage.
Andrew	Or a swimming pool kit.
Jane	Or a folded up football pitch.
Andrew	Or a washing machine.
Narrator	As they looked, a strange thing happened. The present was opening up!

(Music, lights)

Andrew	I've never heard of a present opening itself before. It's weird, if you ask me.
Jane	I think it wants us to look inside.
Narrator	The children peered inside.
Andrew	It's full of darkness and stars . . .
Jane	And a street with lamposts.

(Tape track 1: Carol singers. Congregation join in.)

Andrew	And there's people, coming this way!

(Carol singers climb out, walk to centre aisle and sing 'We wish you a merry Christmas'.)

Jane	Wait till I tell my friends that I had carol singers in one of my presents.
Andrew	Do you think there's room for anything else inside?
Jane	Of course not, stupid. It's only a box. (THUNDER) Oh sorry, present, I didn't mean to upset you.
Andrew	I think this is a real Christmas present. It's got Christmas inside.
Jane	And Christmas means carol singers.
Andrew	Come on everyone, let's ask the Christmas present what else is inside.
All	Christmas present, Christmas present, what else is inside?

(Tape track 2: Shopping. Shoppers climb out and do their chant.)

Andrew	That's the bit of Christmas that makes the grown-ups grumpy.
Jane	And the children pests!
Andrew	Perhaps we ought to make Christmas simpler next year.
Jane	Yes, then we could enjoy it without tiring ourselves out.
All	Christmas present, Christmas present, what else is inside?

(Tape track 3: Postman Pat. Postman climbs out and delivers letters to everyone.)

Andrew	That's a lovely part of Christmas.
Jane	It helps our friends know we are thinking about them and haven't forgotten them.
Andrew	I can see hills in there now, and it feels quite cold.
All	Christmas present, Christmas present, what else is inside?

(Tape track 4: James Herriot theme music. Sheep come bleating out and scatter.)

Andrew	Hey! Hold on! This is getting out of control – there's sheep everywhere! Whatever will Mum say when she sees her carpet?
Narrator	The children tried to catch the sheep. But the sheep didn't want to be caught at all.
Jane	It's no good. Sheep are even worse than rabbits to catch.
Andrew	What we need are some shepherds. Are there any shepherds inside this Christmas present?
Jane	Yes, of course there are – the shepherds who were watching their sheep on the hills outside Bethlehem. Here they come, thank goodness.

(Shepherds climb out and collect sheep together. Tape track 5: 'Ding dong! merrily on high'. Congregation join in.)

Andrew	I can hear music and the box is full of light.
All	Christmas present, Christmas present, what else is inside?

(Angels climb out and walk around. Angels sing the 'Clap Hands Gloria'. Congregation join in.)

Jane	I remember now. The angels told the shepherds about Jesus being born.
Andrew	What did the shepherds do?
Jane	They left the hillside and ran down to Bethlehem.
Andrew	Who looked after their sheep?
Jane	I expect it was the angels.

(Shepherds give their crooks to the angels and run off. Angels guard sheep. Sheep sing 'God has put his angels'. Congregation join in second time.)

Andrew	The Christmas present is playing music again. Listen.

All	Christmas present, Christmas present, what else is inside?

(Tape track 6: 'Silent night'. Congregation join in. One cherub climbs out and runs to collect Mary, Joseph and Jesus, who have been sitting in the congregation.)

Andrew	Look, the box is closing.
Jane	So Jesus must be the very centre of Christmas.

(Everyone gathers round and sings 'Jesus, Jesus'.)

Andrew	I don't want Jesus to come out just at Christmas.
Jane	He doesn't. Jesus is God himself, and God is with us all the time. It's just that we don't always take any notice of him.
Andrew	Our world certainly needs his love.

(All sing 'Shine Jesus, shine'.)

(Everyone gathers round the crib, led by Mary, Joseph and Jesus.)

Suggestion for prayer

Lord, our God,
we know you are here all the time
and not just at Christmas.
Thank you for your love
which goes on and on.
Help us not to pack you away
when this Christmas is over,
but enjoy living in your company
every day of the year.
Amen.

As the Christmas tree lights are switched on:

Leader	The Christmas tree is an evergreen tree.
All	And the love of our God goes on for ever and ever!
Leader	The Christmas tree lights shine bright in the dark.
All	And the love of our God shines bright for ever and ever!
Leader	May the love and faithfulness of God fill our lives and our homes.
All	Faithful, loving God, we welcome you!

Everyone claps.

A candle-lit birthday cake is brought on, and everyone sings 'Happy birthday to Jesus'.

Slices of cake are shared out as everyone goes home.

THE TIME MACHINE

–A Christmas Play

To be performed at

on

All Welcome!

Script Four

The Time Machine

SETTING

Children wrapping their Christmas presents find a friendly time machine has visited them and invites them on a journey. They climb aboard and are swept back into the past until they are at the beginning of time, and watch the creation taking place.

The time machine takes them forward to see the unfolding of God's plan, and leading eventually to Jesus being born. They begin to understand God's love for his creation and his willingness to lay his glory aside in order to save us.

All the action is cued by the hidden voice of the time machine.

CAST LIST

- The time machine
- 2 or 3 children to be in the time machine
- Sound and light effects group
- Creation group
- Prophets (3)
- Gabriel
- Mary
- Joseph
- Jesus

PRODUCTION GUIDELINES

1 The time machine

It is possible to make a very impressive time machine using the diagram below. The basic shape can be created from cardboard fixed round two chairs and decorated with tinsel and tinfoil during the workshop.

A microphone needs to be fixed up at the time machine, so that the children can read their words into it. There are deliberately no words for the children to say before they reach the time machine.

The time machine's voice is from a hidden adult using another microphone, or a radio mike. This person needs to be sitting where he/she can watch the action so that he/she can ad lib if necessary to remind people of what they are supposed to be doing. (eg. 'I think I can see some animals, now; it looks as if they're walking in a procession!')

Give the time machine and the children their scripts early, so they have a chance to familiarise themselves with the text. Let them practise with the microphones as well, paying particular attention to volume and pace. Remind everyone to speak slower than usual.

2 The creation

This sequence can be accompanied either by taped music (such as Stravinsky's *Rite of Spring* and Saint-Saëns' *Carnival of the Animals*) or by

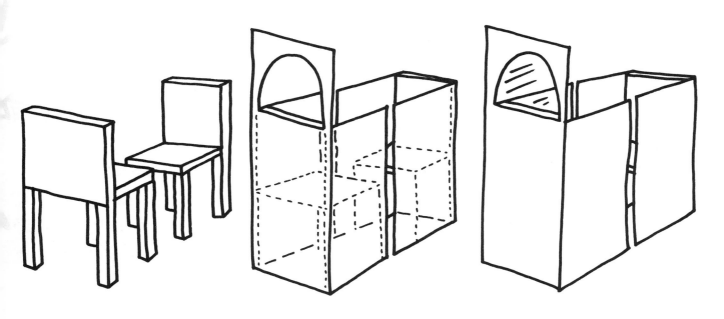

home-grown music from keyboard and percussion instruments. This will depend on the talents and interests of leaders available.

The creation sequence is as follows:

Light – lights gradually come on after the darkness during the time-journey. The children are lying very still.

Land and sea – the children crawl slowly to two pre-arranged places and settle there. Two children from each clump of land unfold a length of blue cloth, or a blue sheet, and wave it between the groups.

Plants – one group of children gradually grows into a forest of trees. They have brightly coloured fruits dangling over their arms. Another group grows and holds up flower heads made from decorated paper plates.

Sun, moon and stars – two adults come and stand in the front of the centre aisle holding lighted candles. A child beside them hands out candles. Six children (three either side) take candles and light them, carrying them down and round the church. A sun and moon, made of foil-covered card fixed on canes, are carried around with the 'stars'.

Fish and birds – the birds, wearing bird hats and brightly coloured clothes, 'fly' all around the church. At the same time, the other children wave blue and green crêpe paper streamers, and the fishes, made of glitter and/or foil covered card, are walked up and down between the streamers.

Animals and humans – the children hop, jump, squirm, run and lumber their way around the church, making appropriate noises.

3 The time journeys

It is most effective to have a small set of disco lights for this. Otherwise, use the ordinary lighting imaginatively, varying the places lit up and the frequency of the flashing. I realise this is not terribly good for lights, but as it is only a one-off occasion it should do no harm.

When the journey begins, everyone in the congregation hums. One group of children 'beep'. One group make a higher 'ning, ning, ning' sound. It should fit in a bit like this:

MMMMMMMMMMMMMMMMMMMM
BEEP BEEP BEEP BEEP BEEP BEEP
NING NING NING NING NING NING

4 Sounds from the past

You only need short fragments of sound for this, so the pieces you use need to be easily recognisable for your congregation. You could use items of local interest, or try these suggestions.

- A snatch from a recent hit.
- A classic, such as something from The Beatles.
- A steam engine. (You can borrow these tapes from the library or a train enthusiast.)
- Either an 'all clear' siren, or gunfire, from a war film.
- Horses' hooves, made from coconut halves.
- Crackling of a fire.
- Battle of Hastings. Sound of metal knives clashing.
- Rumbling of volcanos, made from rattling a large sheet of card or a large tin tray.

5 Crowd control

Use stickers of different colours, given out as the children register, to split the children into groups for the craftwork and creation sequence. It is easiest if the fish make the fish, and the plants their fruit and so on. These props are placed spread out along the front for the children to pick up at the right time. It helps everything to move smoothly if each group of children has a young leader (either the oldest in the group, or a 12 to 15 year old) who keeps them together and reminds them of what to get and when.

The stickers can also be used to ensure that the children are already grouped for the fighting and arguing mime and 'freezing' section after the creation.

6 Music

(For a complete list of sources, please see page 60)

Fishes of the ocean
Never let Jesus into your heart
Be still

Script

The Time Machine

(A tape of Christmas carols is being played, and Jessica and Max are wrapping up their Christmas presents. Suddenly the music stops.)

All   Beep, beep, beep, beep.

(The children stop still and look around. The beeping stops, the carols carry on where they left off and the children shrug and go back to their parcels. Suddenly the music stops again.)

All   Beep, beep, beep, beep.

(The children stop again and look around.)

Time Machine   (Clears throat) Yes, that's right, you did hear something beeping. Can't you see me? – I'm over here!

(The children walk curiously across to the time machine. They peer at it.)

Time Machine   Well, I don't bite, you know. You can get in if you like. I'm getting tired of waiting. You took ages over your fish fingers at lunch. I was beginning to think we'd never get started.

Max   This is a time machine, Jess. It's a talking time machine! Hello, Time Machine, I'm Max and this is my sister Jessica.

Time Machine   Most honoured to make your acquaintance, Max and Jessica. Welcome aboard.

(The children climb in.)

Jessica   Hello, Time Machine. Sorry you had to wait for us. Max always takes ages over his fish fingers. Where are we going?

Max   What about our Christmas presents? We have to get them wrapped up this afternoon.

Time Machine   Oh that's alright. Time outside stopped when you climbed in, so when we get back you won't have lost any time at all. We're going backwards in time and, if you're ready, we'll start straight away. Hold tight, here we go!

(Lights flash on and off, and the sound effects hum and beep their way into the past. Over the noises you can hear a series of sounds from the past.)

Time Machine   (Commenting as the sounds progress) That's (this year's) chart topper . . .and now we're back to (a not so recent hit) . . . and here comes a steam engine, I think . . . Ah! that sounds like 1941, to me (war siren) . . . and back to a quieter life with those horses, before cars were invented. Let's speed up a bit, or it'll take us forever to get where we're going.

(Sound effects speed up, and lights flash faster.)

Jessica   I'm feeling dizzy!

Time Machine   Close your eyes if you like! That's the Fire of London we just passed, and here comes the Battle of Hastings, 1066. On we go, full speed now!

(Sound effects and lights speed up more.)

Time Machine   You can't really catch what's happening at this speed, but we're passing the dinosaurs . . . and now the earth is getting warmer and you can smell the sulphur of all the volcanoes . . .we're nearly there; let's slow down.

(The sound and light effects slow down and stop.)

Max	Phew! What a journey! But where are we? I can't see anything at all.
Time Machine	That's because there isn't anything to see. Nothing has been made, yet. We've gone so far back that God hasn't begun making anything.
Jessica	It's so dark and empty.
Time Machine	Wait a minute, something's happening.

(Lights come on (gradually, if possible) accompanied by a shimmer of sound. The creation takes place, while music plays, with children working through the sequence using props they have made in the workshop.)

Song: *Fishes of the ocean (The whole creation dances round the church.)*

Max	What a fantastic world God made! It was such a good idea to fill all that emptiness.
Jessica	Fancy God trusting us to look after it. We let him down when we mess it up, don't we?
Time Machine	Well, because he loves you all, he made you free to choose.
Max	And we don't always choose what's good and right. I know I don't.
Jessica	Sometimes you do, Max. You cleaned out the rabbit when it was my turn last week.
Max	Mum told me to – you had a bad cold, remember?
Time Machine	You still did it, without moaning, Max, and that was good because it was kind and thoughtful. But you're right; although the world is beautiful, people often mess things up. Let's go forward in time a bit, and watch.

(Sounds and lights of the moving time machine. Then they stop. Children are standing in groups all over the church, arguing and fighting. When a cymbal clashes they freeze in these positions.)

Time Machine   There you are. People are always fighting and quarrelling.

Jessica   That must make God sad. Couldn't he get in touch with people and show them how to live better?

Time Machine   That's a very good idea, and God thought of it too. He sent messengers called prophets to explain to the people how he loved them and wanted them to behave. Here's one now.

(A prophet walks up the church, calling out.)

Prophet 1   Listen to God! Love him and love one another!

(The sounds and lights continue)

Time Machine   And here's another.

(Another prophet walks up the church, calling out.)

Prophet 2   Turn from evil and do good. Get ready for God to come to you!

Time Machine   And another!

(A prophet walks up the church, calling out.)

Prophet 3   Make your lives straight. Get ready for God to come to you!

Jessica   Did you hear what he said, Time Machine? He said God was actually going to come to them. How could he do that?

Time Machine   It sounds impossible, doesn't it? Let's go forward in time to about 2000 years ago, and see what God has in mind.

(Sounds and lights of the moving time machine. Then they stop. Gabriel walks up the church.)

Max	Hang on, I know who that is! That's not a prophet – it's the angel Gabriel.
Jessica	Well I suppose Gabriel is still a messenger. It was Gabriel who had a message for Mary, wasn't it?
Max	Here comes Mary, now.

(Mary walks from the front and meets Gabriel.)

Time Machine	Yes, Gabriel is asking Mary to take part in 'Operation Save the World'. God is planning to help people from the inside, so to speak, by living among them as a human person.
Max	Suppose she refuses?

(Mary goes down on one knee and bows her head.)

Jessica	She isn't refusing. Look, she's agreeing to go ahead with it.
Max	Thank goodness!
Time Machine	Yes, indeed we do! Shall we go forward just a matter of months and see what happens?

(Sounds and lights start for the moving time machine. Gabriel leaves Mary and walks back down the aisle. Mary gets up and walks round another way, eventually getting to the back. The children gather at the front with their creation craftwork. Sounds and lights stop. The Christmas carol we heard at the beginning comes on again. Mary, Joseph and Jesus walk up to the front, led by Gabriel, and stand in the centre of the creation.)

Jessica	That's right, I remember this. Jesus was born in Bethlehem. What happened when he grew up? Did God manage to save the world by being in it as a human?
Time Machine	Yes, he did. Jesus showed everyone God's love in a way they had never been able to see it before.

Max	I wish he hadn't done it so long ago. I'd like to meet him now.
Time Machine	Time isn't a problem for God, Max. We *can* meet him now – he's just as much alive now as he was then! But a word of warning – if you once let Jesus into your life, you will never be quite the same again!

Song: *Never let Jesus into your heart*

Max	Well, it sounds as if life with Jesus is going to be quite an adventure.
Jessica	Yes, I wonder what other good ideas God has in mind?
Time Machine	Who knows! One thing is certain, though. You can talk to him any time and he's always there listening. I've travelled over the whole of time and, wherever I go, God is always there.

Song: *Be still, for the presence of the Lord*

(*During the singing everyone gathers round the crib, or turns to face it. Everyone is led in prayer.*)

Suggestion for prayer

Lord of all time and space,
we want to thank you
for the way you are always with us,
wherever we go
and however old or young we are.
We thank you for being born as a human
and living among us,
showing us what God is like.
Amen.

All   We welcome you into our homes this Christmas.

(The Christmas tree lights are switched on.)

Leader   As our Christmas tree is filled with light

All   Fill us with love for one another.

Everyone claps.

A birthday cake with a lit candle is brought in and everyone sings 'Happy birthday to Jesus'.

Slices of cake are distributed to everyone before they leave.

Source Books for Songs

All the traditional Christmas carols used in the workshops are widely available in various hymn books and carol collections. However, to assist leaders we give below a list of possible source books for the more modern songs which have been suggested:

The Bethlehem Herald

See him lying on a bed of straw (by Michael Perry)
© Michael Perry/Jubilate Hymns

Hymns Old & New (New Century – Catholic edition)
Hymns Old & New (New Anglican edition)
Songs of Fellowship
Mission Praise 2

Our (my) God is so big (author unknown)

Children's Praise
Church Family Worship
Junior Praise
Songs of Fellowship for Kids

The sky is filled (by Mick Gisbey)
© Kingsway's Thankyou Music

Ishmael tape
Songs of Fellowship Book 5
Songs of Fellowship for Kids

Starbirth

Father God, you love me (by Paul Crouch and David Mudie) © Daybreak Music

Kids' Praise '93
The Big Book of Spring Harvest Kids' Praise

For God so loved the world (by John L Hardwick)
© Daybreak Music

Kids' Praise '93
The Big Book of Spring Harvest Kids' Praise

The Christmas Present

Clap hands Gloria (by Mike Anderson)
© Mike Anderson

Hymns Old & New (New Century – Catholic edition)
Celebration Hymnal

God has put his angels (by Alison Moon)
© Daybreak Music

Kids' Praise '93
The Big Book of Spring Harvest Kid's Praise
Living on the Edge

Jesus, Jesus (author unknown)
See page 63 for words and music

Shine, Jesus, shine (by Graham Kendrick)
© Make Way Music

Hymns Old & New (New Century – Catholic edition)
Hymns Old & New (New Anglican edition)
Songs of Fellowship
Songs of Fellowship for Kids

The Time Machine

Fishes of the ocean (by Susan Sayers)
© Kevin Mayhew Ltd

See page 61 for words and music

Never let Jesus into your heart (by Susan Sayers)
© Kevin Mayhew Ltd

See page 62 for words and music

Be still (by Dave Evans)
© Kingsway's Thankyou Music

Hymns Old & New (New Century – Catholic edition)
Hymns Old & New (New Anglican edition)
Songs of Fellowship

Acknowledgements and Copyright information

The publishers wish to thank Daybreak Music Ltd, 4 Regency Mews, Silverdale Road, Eastbourne, E Sussex BN20 7AB for permission to include the text of the song *For God so loved the world* © Copyright 1993 Daybreak Music.

We would also like to remind the users of this book that many of the songs suggested are copyright. This must be borne in mind when preparing OHP slides or song sheets. If your church is a member of CCL the copying of most of these songs will be covered by your licence (please check your CCL reference manual for guidance). Alternatively, permission will need to be obtained from the relevant copyright holder.

Fishes of the ocean

1. Fish-es of the o-cean and the birds of the air, they all de-

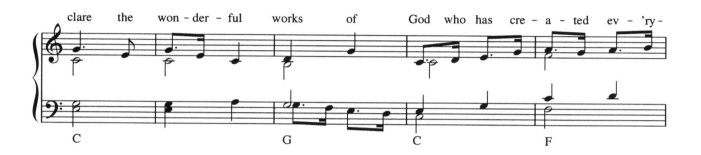

clare the won-der-ful works of God who has cre-a-ted ev-'ry-

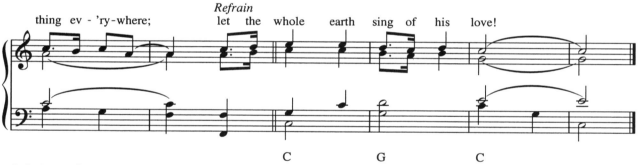

thing ev-'ry-where; *Refrain* let the whole earth sing of his love!

Refrain may be used as an introduction

2. Apples in the orchard and the corn in the field,
   the plants all yield their fruit in due season,
   so the generosity of God is revealed;

3. Energy and colour from the sun so bright,
   the moon by night; the patterns of stars all
   winking in the darkness on a frosty cold night;

4. Muddy hippopotamus and dainty gazelle,
   the mice as well, are all of his making,
   furry ones, and hairy ones, and some with a shell;

5. All that we can hear and everything we can see,
   including me, we all of us spring from
   God who cares for each of us unendingly;

Words and music: Susan Sayers
© 1986 Kevin Mayhew Ltd

Never let Jesus into your heart

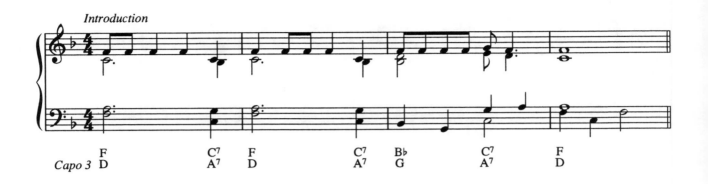

Introduction

F   C⁷ F   C⁷ B♭   C⁷   F

Capo 3 D   A⁷ D   A⁷ G   A⁷   D

1. Ne-ver let Je-sus in - to your heart un - less you are pre-pared for change. If you

C⁷ F   C⁷ B♭   C⁷   F

A⁷ D   A⁷ G   A⁷   D

once let Je-sus in - to your heart you will ne-ver be the same a - gain. He will

B♭   F B♭   F⁷ B♭   C⁷   F

G   D G   D⁷ G   A⁷   D

turn your weak-ness in - to strength and suf-fer-ing in - to joy. He will

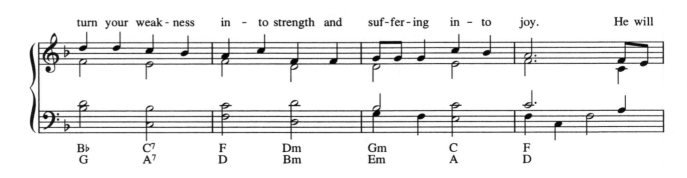

B♭   C⁷   F   Dm   Gm   C   F

G   A⁷   D   Bm   Em   A   D

wash you clean as the drift-ing snow, give peace no-one can de-stroy.

Bb / G   C / A   F / D   Bb / G   C7 / A7   F / D

2. Never let Jesus into your heart
   unless you are prepared for change.
   If you once let Jesus into your heart
   you will never be the same again.
   He will use your gifts to help this world.
   Put you where he can use you best.
   In return he'll love and he'll comfort you.
   In him your heart will find rest.

Words and music: Susan Sayers

Jesus, Jesus

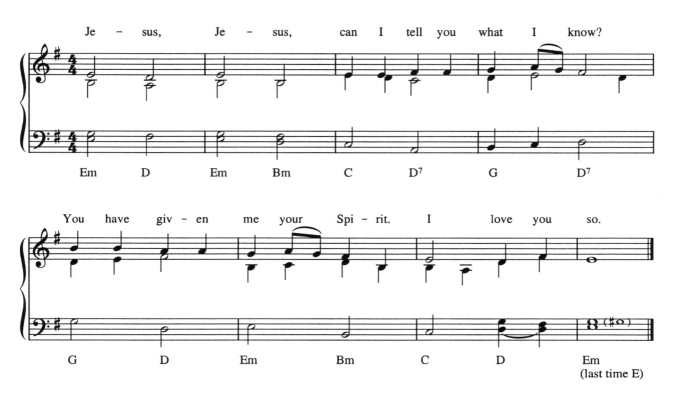

Je - sus, Je - sus, can I tell you what I know?

Em   D   Em   Bm   C   D7   G   D7

You have giv-en me your Spi-rit. I love you so.

G   D   Em   Bm   C   D   Em
(last time E)

Text and music: Unknown

Notes